NOSTALGIA FOR A WORLD
WHERE WE CAN LIVE

Crab Orchard Series in Poetry
OPEN COMPETITION AWARD

NOSTALGIA FOR A WORLD WHERE WE CAN LIVE

POEMS BY

MONICA BERLIN

Crab Orchard Review &
Southern Illinois University Press
Carbondale

Southern Illinois University Press
www.siupress.com

21 20 19 18   4 3 2 1

The Crab Orchard Series in Poetry is a joint publishing venture of
Southern Illinois University Press and *Crab Orchard Review*. This series
has been made possible by the generous support of the Office of the
President of Southern Illinois University and the Office of the Vice
Chancellor for Academic Affairs and Provost at Southern Illinois Uni-
versity Carbondale.

Editor of the Crab Orchard Series in Poetry: Jon Tribble
Judge for the 2017 Open Competition Award: Adrian Matejka

Library of Congress Cataloging-in-Publication Data
Names: Berlin, Monica, 1973– author.
Title: Nostalgia for a world where we can live : poems /
    by Monica Berlin.
Description: Carbondale : Crab Orchard Review & Southern
    Illinois University Press, 2018. | Series: Crab Orchard series
    in poetry
Identifiers: LCCN 2018010149 | ISBN 9780809336838 (pbk. : alk.
    paper) | ISBN 9780809336845 (e-book)
Classification: LCC PS3602.E75776 N67 2018 | DDC 811/.6—dc23
LC record available at https://lccn.loc.gov/2018010149

Printed on recycled paper. ♻

This paper meets the requirements of ANSI/NISO Z39.48-1992
    (Permanence of Paper) ∞

For E—always, & on & on

. . . and the future, the future
—Inger Christensen

CONTENTS

Nostalgia for a World Where We Can Live   1

What a year looks like: drenched. So soggy here. So much   5

No apples on the apple tree this summer, & if there were   7

Another late summer early quiet blue-skied morning, my son   9

On either end of this year, on either end of every goddamn year,   11

When we turn the calendar's page, my little boy looking   12

The dark flurry of another morning purred   14

This afternoon the sky's making the kind of promises it can   15

Days the hours are no more fact than the unbelievable   17

Sometimes being *here* is like   19

To scale, yes, days to scale, even when they grow so cluttered   22

Just before the blood draw the other morning, I filled in small   24

We loved the rush hour most, the cars suit-filled, briefcase-heavy,   29

Today, three flights up, with my whole body, I lifted   30

Some disasters are given names, others called after   31

The truth is I have trouble forgiving most things, although I've never minded 32

By rote the body learns nearly everything, after   34

It's true. There are places we'd rather be   35

Not quite another season, but almost, & on the window ledges,   36

How I wish more things I read I misread, like the bodies in the mine   37

Because you're still in another time zone disparate things   38

The problem is the revolving door, this   39

Because I wasn't thinking *peninsula*   41

If there's a joke more complicated than "knock-knock," more   43

Too lazy to lip-read in noisy rooms, the other night   44

A kind of stutter, that over &   45

Down the hall the accordion man turns into a door   47

Long before the horse pulls up lame there is the matter   48

Back to this wind, up against it even,   51

The linens soften, now threadbare, just as I'm waking, small, in this   54

When morning was almost unrecognizable as morning   55

What the wind kicks up, what the waters trouble, even   56

The forecast's calling for flurries tomorrow, & worry   58

At the new year, in the dark, I watched time   59

The lesson tonight nothing less than   60

In this, this snow-brightened light of a near-spring morning, I think of his glass   61

How quickly the body, when asked, forgets   62

Stay mouthed through   63

How quiet every end when it comes, briefest glimpse of a future   64

If all the love we'll know is the kind of love   65

Because all day the sky held back   66

Not only the night   67

Notes   71

Acknowledgments   73

NOSTALGIA FOR A WORLD
WHERE WE CAN LIVE

NOSTALGIA FOR A WORLD WHERE WE CAN LIVE

The Monday I first hear the body count my father
would've just turned sixty-four. Rocking the baby

to sleep I wonder how I'd introduce them. This
might be the year he's been my dead father as long

as he was not. That I've lost track only occurs to me
because my father loved that folksy Steve Goodman

"City of New Orleans" train song. I can't call up his voice,
but remember the needle skimming vinyl, my father

laying hands against the speaker—that record player
more cabinet than turntable—to hear it.

Four years before this body count, numbers scroll
the bottom of the TV, the totaling dead change

by the hour. You, working a murder trial, don't
know I can't turn away. From our upstairs

bathroom, late at night, I watch the blur
of bakers in a doughnut shop one block over.

At this distance, the storefront lit up recalls
a Hopper painting. But the Hoppers I love

hold those women turning away, & a bed or a chair.
Tugging the blinds I watch everything fill with tolls.

Each body piling up belonged to a name or once
longed or was held. That's true, right?

Everybody's head once cupped in the palm
of another? My friend N lived

across from the doughnut shop, his willpower
impressive. When I called him a holdover

from another time, a throwback, I meant it
as a compliment. I'm only thinking of this

because N & his wife grew a vegetable garden
shaped like a small boat. In the morning,

everyone at work, I walk the baby by
in his stroller & imagine climbing aboard,

setting us adrift, although I still can't swim.
One of my mom's greatest disappointments

might've been her children always afraid
to get their faces wet. Her watery grace

stilted, standing shoreside, begging us to just touch
our toes in the lake. My father made excuses, not wanting

to leave his hearing aid on a towel. If my son ever asks
after my great disappointment, how to ensure

he never thinks *I was*? How to hand him this world?
What I meant about N was I hope to know him

in other times. He remembers to hold the door
open for others. He rises from his chair

when his wife enters. He collects broken things
& fixes them. He makes soup from bones.

—

WHAT A YEAR LOOKS LIKE: DRENCHED. SO SOGGY HERE. SO MUCH

for a want of overcast sky. It's here, already, again & soaking

everything. There's no telling what won't be
water-stained come summer's end. No telling how high

the watermark. Or where what's spilling over might crest.
So, it's true I've been distracted by how green

everything has stayed: no midsummer scorching
of anything this year; no delirious afternoon spent

in a shiny daydream of snow. What distracts is more
than the need for sleeves. Like my little boy,

I'm afraid of forgetting. Before another heartbreaking decade
turns he won't remember those quiet, wet years. Maybe

for the best. He was four months old, asleep against
my chest, when that tsunami bore down; we were finishing

thank-you notes for his first birthday when levees gave way
in St. Bernard Parish. Or that other summer the Mississippi nearly

drowned this flat-landed kind of forever forever before he started
to ask why so much water everywhere. Let him never know how

much his small body pressed against my own—the memory of that
holding—tangled up with so much ruin. Let him never recall

the news footage I watched again & again while I rocked him. Not
the way we'd curl together in the soft light of each of those days.

Not the way he looked, smalled, when he stood beside his father,
beneath my office window, three flights down, calling up to me,

or on a late-season beach all our own, a lighthouse off
in the distance somehow looming over him. Not even the way another

night in a tall hotel I woke to find him sitting on the sill staring out
into the cityscape of electricity & thought, My god, he's going on

without us. He'll go on without us. None of it—not any of it—saved
for some scrapbook. Even you are slipping away, these months without

you, so that now you're just someone else he's spent the time he knows
best—today—without. Let me get this down. Maybe twenty-five years ago,

surely another lifetime, the north branch of the Chicago River tripped
its banks, poured into the street where I lived. That we walked

everywhere in our wellies until the water subsided must be true,
but I can't quite believe it. Instead, this: I thought it was our fault—

another ten-year flood—for playing in the hydrants all summer long,
for taxing the drainage system. I'm only thinking of that water

because of this water, or maybe because it has no memory—likely
all drugged on Versed just before it rushes in. Land remembers.

Not us. Not us with our bodies more liquid than soil, more fluid
than certain, more permeable than anything.

blossoms in the spring—those petals falling like snow, all

in one day—I don't recall. No apples rotting on the grass
either, though, so let me be clear this isn't complaint so much

as notation, all it's ever really been now that I
think about it, just a record kept in some variation

on a little book of days. Maybe it was all that water—
the frozen ground warming, turned porous, turned sponge,

then unable to take on any more; maybe it was the scorching
heat that followed—days so dry light miraged every street

corner, miraged every inch of distance where we stood.
I'm no horticulturist, but what I know for sure: the only perennial

this year was invasive, the only thing reliably consistent
was how we didn't know where next the disaster

only that it would come, inevitable like everything.
It's a ghost town here again, & there are ghosted

towns everywhere—towns designated as such by economics
or migration, made such by weather's furious power, made

ghost by progress. In a book I'm reading there includes
an index of towns swallowed up by the river, cities flooded,

levees breached or blown wide open. Spread out before me,
a map made before so much of this country moved itself to crowd

itself citywide, before we left doors swinging open, windows leaking
rain that would come & come. So much of it doesn't exist

now. All those places—now charted Xs of tumbleweed—
echo. Abandoned tracks connecting your nowhere with any other

nowhere, even a town called Waterproof—which would make some
people laugh, but not us. Our mouths turn down. What I mean

about *here*, what I meant to say about *here*, is that even though traffic
rumbles by, even though the signals at the crossing engage dozens

of times each day, even though the population holds mostly
steady: we are alone here again. All the leavings always the same

& always at the same time: months of last things,
those bags packed & set in the foyer, boxes sent

via post, cupboard shelves wiped bare, a truck waiting
half-empty on the curb. Maybe what I mean to say

is that every town is a ghost town. Maybe what I mean
to say is that I've come to see all the names we might

recognize destruction by. We sometimes call it *the river*,
on faith. We sometimes call it *holy*, in awe. We might

sometimes, stupidly, call it *love*. Or we might sometimes
call it *man-made*, shaking our heads in embarrassment.

ANOTHER LATE SUMMER EARLY QUIET BLUE-SKIED MORNING, MY SON

next to me where I'd fallen asleep watching
news, says *It's all weather.* Not half

-awake we stare at the eastern seaboard waist-deep
that later will power up generators, peel tape from windows,

turn at last to look down at what's rising instead
of up toward the sky, & we'll cross

twice the Mississippi, still swollen, although there's no rain
to speak of. On the bridge that carries us over

that fierce Old Man, I think of the Hudson,
how we leaned together in a small boat & he said

The water's made of paper. If only—but then I remember
all the falling sheets, their imprint,

that other September in that same New York,
that blizzard's resilience. How we can say *drought*

& *flood* on the same day in this same country
& mean both—even now the river's still

high & the ground choked & the coast's nowhere
to go. How we practice these words again & again only

to come up absent any worthwhile logic. How we just keep
going under. Or how the world looks to him:

any day's given turbulence, sense of scale, the always-roiling
perspective, the proportions unstable, the front-porch steps

a lake where a house once stood, the highways'
gaping fissures, the missing miles, those rivers made

of paper, or a boy—his age—carrying a small cat
through streets made tributary.

ON EITHER END OF THIS YEAR, ON EITHER END OF EVERY GODDAMN YEAR,

there are days without. Not quite a gap in whatever they call it, the space-

time continuum or circadian rhythms or the tidal pull of every single thing,
not quite, but noticeable enough to know what's not here, that others are not here,

that on this bricked stretch of aging birch & maple, in this windowed house
far from any ocean, we're each alone, together. I don't dream any of you

here, not yet, although in sleep, I puzzle things back—which I do
sometimes—though other things piece apart. Before I ever saw the gesture

of my son's body in the sonographer's monitor, I'd tell his father we were
dreaming him whole every single day. After the first ultrasound,

after the specialists, I never said the phrase again. As if the very words might've
been to blame for what my body did to his. Listen, I can't quite

get it all right: the correct order of an adage, calling up the grocery list left
on the kitchen table, the distance from street to curb, how to say you

have meant the world to me. Now, in dreams, everyone limbless.
It's so transparent, I know, but I can't help myself. In one, the boy

I could love raised what remained of his arm & grazed my cheek
with what was left, stroked my jawbone. I remember the timbre

of my dream-whisper when I held him to my body, touched his fine hair,
told him of the map the nerves make, what they remember for us, the way

the chest can become a home to all those lost fingertips, the prints
of each of us, the way the heart can hold every missed & missing hand.

hard at the sky pressed up against the window, asks
Where is it? again & again.

Impatience keeps fraying
the gray of each morning to distract him,

to pull him from that frame & back into the room
I'm staring out into, wishing away another month, another

season, these days I'm lucky to have & down on my knees over.
I know what he's waiting for, what will come & come

so that weeks from now in the longest month, he'll beg
for the greening as inevitable as everything.

As far away. But first this: this in a flat
in the city, & there, in the east-

facing windows, cars sloshing down Southport, lights wrapped up
each tree, that low rumble I'll remember all my life

calls up the name of every station, the rise & fall of elevated platforms
I once learned by heart, to pass time or a way. To stave it off

I'd ride, & ride the city to the end of heartbreak, maybe. Another way,
in my ears, with my body. But this day

I'll help him maneuver his first turnstile,
watch his face in the train's window as we head underground, & there,

in the city from which I ran & ran away, I'll understand each thing,
its shape the place holding it—like how a fish grows

to fit the bowl or the pond or the lake or the river.
A fish will. We all will, & do. & so, too, with little boys.

So, too, winter, this day, snow on the shoulders
of our coats. Fearless, he'll stand beside me near the doors, long before

our station, & I'll show him how to plant his balance
in the lurches, to shift the starts, the stops, the going & going on,

the curves & then: the first time I'd released my hold. How that easing
off of hands made me always want to stand still by the doors of a train

that moves & moves. That urge, always. That letting go.

up to my neck, the light just coming on, another

day's tiny disasters waiting to knock against us,
to knock us over. In beds we're most reminded

of our smallness, coming in & out of sleep
to the sound of the scraping plow, the garbage truck's

heaving, a wail of sirens. Once, curled up & sheltering
against that raining city in an oversized hotel room,

I watched dancers in their studio blocks away,
their pirouettes, their pliés. Even at a distance

how unbearable that grace, how clumsy we are
even not moving. & this, what's most

worried the finish from: our own
proportions to the rest of the things

in our way. I'm not saying we spend our whole lives
palm-scraping slick cement, or tumbling down,

or cornering the bed's frame, although these days—
rough-shinned, bruised-up—& now winter

refusing to ease. In this brisk, want: something
handheld, manageable; my body, held tight;

a month pocket-sized, like summer
in a jar; like my once-small

speck of a boy before he really was,
like miniature, like nearly invisible; snow like

someone's idea of snow, some dream of snow.

THIS AFTERNOON THE SKY'S MAKING THE KIND OF PROMISES IT CAN

all too well keep, & us? Still leisure-clad in sleep, still bearing

against the worn-down of another week spent,
just another & another stretch, another hurdle, this

& another that to check ourselves off against, & my son flops
small against me—although his small no longer so & mine

growing smaller, our bodies more similar these days,
his inching up to me. He says, *I can't think*

what to do because my head is full of snow. He says, *I can only
think snowsnowsnow.* O, Baby, I think, that's all

there'll ever be, that whitening-out of every last thing.
My mouth frosted over can't quite tell this

truth, so wide, bare. Although I'm beside him,
I'm distracted by news, again, all the tremors

of the earth that remind me to promise him
everything: no more burying alive of bodies, no more

bodies lost on the roads now covered with snow
or not covered with snow, no more small

heartaches, no more endless ones.
When we flushed his first pet, he wondered if

in the ocean everyone who'd lost or been lost
would be found again. *Under all that water?*

he asked, a little afraid. He leans today
into my shoulder & I'm making the crossing

to other hemispheres only to find water rising,
buildings caving in, us

on our knees although we no longer remember
words, our breath holding

please. Our days shrinking, the kilogram, even
planets, everything

we think we know—. How unalterable
shifts & beside me & he'll be gone.

& maybe, like writing a letter
because you think my god, someone—,

something—, maybe my little boy is
trying to right the days, his head full

of snow. To clear a path, he'll have to
dig out.

DAYS THE HOURS ARE NO MORE FACT THAN THE UNBELIEVABLE

fact of the news that tells us, again, the earth shifted

on its axis—the length of a day shortened again, not
the exact number of milliseconds lost that were also lost

after the quaking in Chile, but a millisecond feels so small,
they're close enough. Days like these, you know? Days

the kindergarten on the hill is lucky to be structurally sound;
the bus already full of children running on time, only too late.

When the black wall of water rushes in & the whole thing
ignites—those children spared the caving, the collapsing,

the burying, but not this other thing—. &
when they're found, their bodies

huddled together in the husk of that bus, parts
of the country have already moved thirteen feet eastward.

What can I say, consumed as I am by my not thinking,
Thank god it wasn't me or my baby, but instead thinking, My god,

those children were someone's children? Or days
the poet just back from Haiti tells me, *It's always horrible,*

but we sometimes survive. Who tells me, *What I saw*
in Port-au-Prince changed everything. Who says, *It's all still*

rubble. Who says, *It's all still gone & still going, & we still go on.*
But for how long? After I tell him about the milliseconds,

how I think it's geography saying disaster is always
disaster, we sit awhile not talking. Or days any

of us will walk into the wind together, for miles, not
talking, your hat blown off & grabbed just before

it topples, your hat now held to your chest. Maybe
you're thinking about the sound plates of the earth must

make when they move a country thirteen feet eastward.
I'm thinking about the sound of the river of trains we're crossing

over, wondering who first called it that, wondering how
any of this will end. I'm thinking about those parents gone

to collect their children at what was once the corner stop
& finding only their huddling, singed bones.

SOMETIMES BEING *HERE* IS LIKE

living—no, sometimes *here* is living on

a fault line, waiting for the next
tremor, & trying to keep

all that's guarded
from tumbling down. To not be the one

to say *hey, why don't we move
those breakables?* As if he understood

that shudder this morning
my little boy said *there are things to do*

*about disaster sometimes & things we can't
do about disaster sometimes, but the only thing*

that will save Haiti is our hearts. I'm omitting
some context here. Sure, he's smart,

that tender, but there was a fund-raiser
at his school, hearts made

of construction paper & strung
together—an easily torn tethering

born out of a holiday
we're all skeptical of—to save

people we won't be able to save.
It was how he said *disaster,* as if

understanding for the first time
that the world makes ruin out of all of us.

For the first time his choice of words
not hyperbolic. Not *catastrophe*. Not *worst*.

Not *never*. No ill-suited, dramatic name given
to something easily forgotten

assigned out of the fictions we learn
to build language around.

The first paragraph he ever uttered
began *once upon a time*. We were driving

a stretch of road we drove often, winter
coming round the corner. I watched his mouth

move over the sounds, those oldest of clauses
in the rearview mirror. Around us the fields

turning toward a starkness held at bay.
I thought then I'd never not hear

his voice in my ears at the start of any story.
Already though it's gone: his small breaths between

words, those palated shapes of letters.
When yesterday turned

late-season blizzard, we built
a house, iced the joinery to hold firm,

tuck-pointed every crevice, mortared each
faux brick. When we thatched the roof

with snow frosting, it started slipping.
Slow & then, then the walls

began to cave. He didn't quite
say it before he grabbed the spatula.

He didn't quite whisper anything—
his mouth full of sugar. In my hands

I was trying to hold everything up, keep it
together. I pressed hard & the trash can gave

way: our miniature collapsing, everything
folding in, sweet-snow-covered, & done for.

no proportion seems possible. Or days to climb, as in height,

like these days: so much stacked-up news teetering near
the table's edge. Days of which there have been many,

too many, & no good way to settle in or brace
against or choose. So, today, reverse chronological,

the months unwound backward, a whole season of sorrow
inverted. A decision made not out of some practicality or

to optimize speed—easier to skip the letters when you
haven't yet read to what the letters refer—but because

yesterday, I watched my little boy walk backward down
the galleyed room of our local bookstore, egged on

by the clerk, then backward out the door & down the street,
all the way to what he trusted was our car, asking only that I warn

him of an obstacle if an obstacle were to suddenly sneak up,
him reflecting off all the windows of all the stores we passed,

all those stores selling things I've never wanted & can't imagine,
for the life of me, who would—all those shiny things, all those things

just to provide a gathering of dust, reminders of our emptiness.
They're all obstacles, I thought, & then, My god, what kind

of obstacle? His body windowed & moving away down the street, he
never took his eyes off mine. How much I once longed for

new angles, upside down on a couch imagining walking
would-be-ceiling made floor, stepping over thresholds, turning

around light fixtures as if they were fountains, as if sculptures.
That ease toward the wonder of gravity or direction,

like birds know, like you know—that altered vista.
So, I read a whole season in reverse, trying out what makes

more creased the news' fold before it unfolds: first spring, then
winter; first radiation seeping into the groundwater, then

the breach; first the fierce ocean grown miles, then land
resettling around it; first memorials; first grief; first recovery,

then the wound. Days like this. First the obstacle, then
the grown boy walking backward, then the boy learning to

walk, then the boy held for the first time. First the epitaph,
then the outcome, then the hopeful naming of each

predicament, last the now-foreshadowy beginnings
of every single thing.

circles on a form, rating likelihood on a scale of one to five:

how likely I was to notice that *I was aware of the action of my heart
in the absence of physical exertion (e.g., the heart missing a beat)*. No space

allowed to say *I'm always aware of the action of my heart*, always aware
of absence, holes, the turning of a doorknob, a shadow moving

against glass, the light, even imagined, someone going away.
The form didn't ask how often I think about the heart, mine or

yours, or the now-healing poet's in Texas, or the scavenged one
of that beast my friend in Michigan is watching this early morning,

late spring, though the sky's still February despite magnolia petals in
the driveway. There's an opossum here, too, but I ignore his mean,

prehistoric face, cover the trash cans, think instead of the raccoon, that
milder primitive fella, I once saw splayed on the roadside, handlike paws

tucked beneath his chin, as in prayer. It's an image from which I've never
recovered, & this morning, returned again, when, helpless, I watched

a car about to be hit by another in an intersection I always fear, &
helpless to stop it from happening, threw mine into park, felt my hands

rush up to cover my own eyes, as if not-seeing would stop what I couldn't,
would alert someone to the peril of every day, which is one of the impossibilities

of our lives, the things we can't stop, the things just ahead of us on the road,
physics at work, without us, without any of us, just the fierceness

of everything not ours to control. It's too late to say I was trying to be
honest on the form. No sense lying about the heart. But there wasn't room

enough to say how, when I said I'd give the poet mine, I meant it.
No room to say when the poet was wheeled in to surgery, I slipped

under, murmured to a friend passing by, *You know how to pray.* Said, *please.*
What I also didn't say: I once walked into a hospital to find doctors

slamming paddles to my father's chest, the room overturned, his body
stripped bare. Too late to say when my father's heart gave up, &

the doctors had to let it, in me there were no prayers left. Too late:
I never prayed again. But about the prayers of others, the way any

body might, in grief or fear, turn toward prayer, always in the hands,
that tucking in against disaster—? I never know if it's too late,

especially not on a form that leaves no option for a change of heart
—Christ, they're only handing out pens, & cheap ones at that—that

here's the thing about the heart: sometimes it breaks, & we go on;
sometimes it breaks, & we can't go on; sometimes the surgeons

can patch a hole, clear the path to it; sometimes the paddles; sometimes
it takes a boy once in a car on a road to nowhere in Oklahoma somewhere

spilled out on gravel. The problem of the heart: there's no easy way
to repair the one we're given. Only dumb luck or great tragedy, the deepest

sorrows, a head-on crash through an intersection into a tree & an airbag
deploying to protect what will be lifted in a tightly sealed box, then driven

at safe speeds, in a truck, through the night, on an emptied-out highway,
one so desolate that even those thieving roadside critters don't bother

to scour. Everything out of our hands: the trains halted then rerouted
after a collapsed bridge, another empty downtown Main Street razed,

a boy once in a car in Oklahoma, the rivers rising, detours, so many
detours. What more is there? This kind of direct address to the human

heart. These stretches of wide-open forever, scarcely seen or seen again.

—

WE LOVED THE RUSH HOUR MOST, THE CARS SUIT-FILLED, BRIEFCASE-HEAVY,

practicing our balance or weaving through the tired end-of-day
to find those small gaps where we could wedge ourselves.

Never mind if we could hold on, never mind someone
else's elbow just above our sight line—we'd close our eyes

& learn by heart the names of all the stops on all the routes
we ever traveled. All these years later, we can still voice

each conductor—they were human then. How they called out
every station: a long-lost sister, a soldier's return, the welcoming

home, a sorrowful locked door, lights left burning in an otherwise
empty brownstone. Or we loved most the old wooden platforms

on the elevated lines quaking beneath our feet when the express
passed us by, & we'd sometimes hold out our arms to feel that rush

of air with our whole bodies. Or we loved riding the express & the blurred
versions of everyone who could've been us. Or the conductor's

ticket punch, & the conductor's nod, & the conductor, always,
his uniform, his purposefulness, how he'd slip between cars, how

he'd put a hand on shoulders of dozers near their usual stops.
As the cars emptied out, we'd push toward window seats, facing back

-ward, & watch it all go by. What trains know we tried our best to learn:
their mournful whistle, the pressure of time, the pressure of gravity,

how to carry every single weariness without slowing down, how to find
a view—no matter the direction, no matter the size of the frame.

TODAY, THREE FLIGHTS UP, WITH MY WHOLE BODY, I LIFTED

the glass pane, floor to near-ceiling high, sealed for a decade,
& when trying to place the rusty screen, the wind carried it out,

away, all those stories down. Between falling objects & this first
spring afternoon light, I read a tiny book whose title we can't say

because we don't distinguish it from what came just before,
that September date turned pale. All the while, I kept

picking up the phone to ring your house, where you weren't,
to tell my friend, who also wasn't, who's burning it down

one drape at a time—in your absence or because of it—how
suddenly I was what's burning, *this* raging in me. Ruin fingers

its way into everything. On the stairs, where I'd rushed
to be sure no injuries were sustained by the falling, I ran

into a boy I know & led him away to speak of stars, which,
he said, are failing him. I almost took his hand.

the town flattened, the force of fury, the body of water
provoked. We name what we know is advancing
toward us; we tag them with a number when they
surprise. Small disasters of every single day—that wear
us down or that we wear round our shoulders, even in
heat, the ones that remind us how human we are, how
tiny, how much of nothing—go unbaptized, however
tragic. & we don't romanticize heat with names, just
say a month, a year, the region, if we can sputter out
even that, stunned-quiet as we become. Here, although
the corn's already high enough to lean in, to lean over,
there'll be no bumper crop again, this year of no rain.
When the weather broke—no, who am I kidding?—
when it broke us & I told you you heard heart broke,
& I had trouble correcting the slip, that endless heart-
break I can't say aloud for fear of making permanent.
Memorializing. This brittle of our keeps-breaking
hearts. We can't name it hunger, won't call it ruin or
sorry or devastated, not yet, but we could.

birds or eccentric older men, never found reason enough to need to forgive
plumage or spectacle, from the Latin, *to see, behold*, & no need for apology

from any scapula, from the Latin, *shoulder*. I'd never begrudge wingspan.
Never that. But this isn't about feathers or bones, not ornithology

& not what is etymological. No, it's about the unforgivable
in this stretch of brutality. Enough that the fires are burning

everything, a drought-scorched century, heat that goes
on & on. & when I say enough, I mean it. Isn't it

something that we can even get out of bed these days? Arms
heavy with books the other morning, I walked newly paved

sidewalk thinking about progress when a wedge of rock
the size of a fist heaved up from beneath a lawn tractor's treads

& hurled at me. I heard it hit bone before I felt it
in my teeth, watched its path—broken by my body—

change course, before I dropped what was in my hands,
before I understood that skin would be broken, the swelling—.

Forgive the man on the machine, his back turned, his looking
forward. Forgive the machine its clumsy, inevitable ways. Forgive

my body its frailty—how quick to tear. But the rock made weapon?
How to forgive that thing unintended? These days my son's suddenly

scared of the dark—every shadow & hallway, every sound
outside once the sun has gone down. I can't blame him. So much

we can't shoulder. In a house down the block, someone left
open the screen door before the bank came to foreclose. Now

the street full of cats. Now the house empty. Now the padlock.
Now a notice hung in the stripped-bare window.

all. Not by touch. Not even muscle memory. In this town smalled
by proximity to water, slowed by distance to shoreline or tide,
where I've been now longer than I've been anywhere, I've taken
to retraining my body the routes disrupted. Even traffic
patterns—what light, what sign, what turn-only lane—broken.
For months that underpass closed, that overpass going up, &
now another fire, one that guts a half block where once a boy I
loved climbed through a window to open a door for me to walk
through & we knelt together in a kind of light I've spent years
trying to replicate—the closest to holy I've known—& these days,
it's all going up again, closed down again, blocked off or re-
routed, & getting lost to find new ways out is another
complication on an already indecipherably creased map, one
I never thought I'd need to untuck from where it was folded all
those years ago. Which is to say every street I turn down detours.
Which is really to say these days there's no other choice. Which is
to say the more beautiful the building the more flammable.
Which is to say the more delicate the thing the easier it's gone.

IT'S TRUE. THERE ARE PLACES WE'D RATHER BE

although *anywhere but here* is tricky to pin
on the wall map my son & I hung,

pushed thumbtacks into—color-coding
where we've been & soon going & want

very much to someday. Last night *here*
again washed the river from my clothes.

Sometimes it's worth trying to figure out
how to say *this*, how to say *here*, how

to do more than point, how to recognize
what is indisputably true. Other times

impossibility of scale makes all sense
ridiculous. Maybe it all comes down

to perspective. Maybe *anywhere but here* isn't
quite accurate. There is sky & water &

us, all of us, wanting to be somewhere.
There is where we are not. There is

sky & water & us moving toward
a future we're already pushing into, hard.

NOT QUITE ANOTHER SEASON, BUT ALMOST, & ON THE WINDOW LEDGES,

under eaves, at the threshold of every door, insects gather & crowd,

trying to come inside. I don't blame them. So that I can tell you about it,
I've learned to identify each. So I can walk by without cringing, I've swept

them from the porch, vacuumed up their crushed limbs, pulled on gloves
to carry them away. So that I can better respect them, I've memorized

their true names, apologized to each one. I've apologized to my son
for everything, too: *sorry* the litter of their bodies, *sorry* the unrelenting heat,

sorry the roads we didn't drive, *sorry* those trees we lost, *sorry* how quick this
stalled & stalling summer, that winter's coming. Apology is something worth

practicing, & I'm trying to get it right. Because these days there's little in me
that's unashamed—deep howl of sad, the tinny ring in my ears of sorrow—

the stretches of listening to nothing but the train's slow moan & its aching
stretch through town turn longer. Maybe someday I'll forget these days so dry

everything became flammable. Maybe someday I'll forgive the news that kept us
up, fraying at everything's hems. Maybe I'll learn to be grateful for those moments

when my tongue suddenly tasted copper—my body stunned silent or stunned angry
or just stunned & mouthing all the harshness of every damned & beautiful day.

HOW I WISH MORE THINGS I READ I MISREAD, LIKE THE BODIES IN THE MINE

in South Africa or the eleven-mile stretch of the Mississippi closed or more
fires burning. Wish them untrue. Always coming nearly undone is what seems

the seams are doing, & today's no different—another politician speaking
the language of stupid, another hopeless man throwing himself from a bridge,

another sentence—one kind or another—but always that word: sentence.
Lately I've been thinking of planting a tree but I worry about signs,

although I don't know that I believe in them, & about water, there not being
enough, & my luck, & whether it's beauty's false promise that moves us

to plant where there's suddenly no rain, or hubris, or just that silly hope
—the same kind that makes us, still, believe in love or someday or

a good soaking or a new season or that reassures us by scale. After all,
the great river winds 2,552 miles to the Gulf & begins 1,475 feet above

sea level, & what's eleven miles in that? After all, tonight the stars
seem to have come out from where they've been hiding or I finally

thought after all these months to look up from the ground & shouldn't
there be something worthwhile to be said in a sentence about that?

surface. Like how, years ago, a young woman held open

a datebook scribbled over & said, *All my days look
like car accidents.* I hadn't thought to look at the pages.

Or how, lately, my son remakes the world every time
he doesn't know the word spoken, repeating back what

he thinks he heard—*quad* becoming *cloud*, *noose* into *news.*
Don't stop me if I've told you any of this before.

He had one tense for a whole year. Twelve months of
the present verb might almost explain the sound

my mother's shoulders still make in the thirty-year dark, darker,
where she cries for my dead father long before he dies.

Day after car accident–ridden day. It wouldn't matter
if we wanted to, we can't forget everything,

& I'm pretty sure we don't get to choose.
Once, as a very cold & drowsy child, I adjusted

the thermostat as far as it would go. I awoke certain
the house was on fire. I laugh to tell it now, but sometimes

even that heat comes back. Today I tell my son the way
to make a thing not scary is to look completely

at the thing itself. When someone touches my hair I turn
to find a woman I've never seen before. *I just want to feel*

something real again, she says, *sorry*, quickly passing.

THE PROBLEM IS THE REVOLVING DOOR, THIS

city, even you. So, I distract myself with physics
—what allows architects to suspend glass

ledges at the Sears Tower, those window
boxes 1,353 feet in the air. People wanted

to look down, they said. Wanted
to feel part of something. Like those

silly doors, at once somehow inside &
out, these little triangular

pockets of space that hold
the air, contain it, until

the press of someone's body
lets it escape. My son, fascinated,

hasn't started to fear being
wedged in while someone fumbles

words into a cell phone, digs in
a handbag, waits out the rain. He's still

happy to lap round & round.
Before summer ends they'll change

the building's name. Before summer
ends, there'll be other

things to worry about. Like about
this town that's become a door:

it's a problem & not just mine.
In what was once my quirky sketch

of home there were thirty-four plus
the set of pockets. After my son was

born, I made a promise not to close up
a room if it meant being separated

by the hard, dark wood of *not now*. But in this
drafty slip of a place, someone is always

packing, or standing in the threshold, or
walking away. We'll get used to lights left

burning when someone exits
a room—although I hear my father

scolding. We'll grow accustomed
to the shape of so many backs.

BECAUSE I WASN'T THINKING *PENINSULA*

meant anything, was just what

we were calling the place where we were
imagine my surprise when I turned

from staring at the lake on my left to find
water on my right, or when I drove

to the peninsular end & found
lake-sky-lighthouse-bay, all

surrounding what seemed rich,
fertile ground where I stood—vineyards

there, & farms that seemed to grow
every single thing. *Doesn't seem fair,*

a near-stranger says aloud when
he must've overheard my gasp,

that they can have so much while we've so little.
I nod, not really hearing, but days

later can't shake what he meant
to reassure. No fault of geography

or topography, just one of the deep
misfortunes of a world this large. There

are sadnesses everywhere, even there
on that beautiful near-island where

drought spoils their summer
harvest & they're shipping in

from overseas the small fruit
to meet demand for what

they're known for best—signature
cherries, those pies. Even there,

they cast eyes down at the soil,
more dry than in decades, then turn

—still in apology—to that horizon
so spacious it becomes unforgiving.

Even there, what I can't see in
the coming-on-dark is that the light

-house now rests on a bed
of sand, water levels so low this

season & the last & the one before
that, that it turned relic, turned

reminder of what's suddenly gone.
What doesn't seem fair, I would've said

to anyone who'd listen, is how we go on,
keep going on, no matter. How we can keep

convincing ourselves to believe in a *return
to normal* or in love—newlywedded & *at long last*

& the vows *forever* & promised, almost too much
levity—or in all that we measure at the water-

mark, in the yield, or, my god, how we keep
believing we've been spared the worst or that

there'll ever be just the right amount of rain.

nuanced than "So, a horse walks into . . ." I'll miss it, my half listening, the only way I seem to these days, although what I'm other half hearing, I can't be sure—maybe something about pockets or how the post office is dying. Brought to my knees by this day's brightness, I think, Sky, give me more than some promise of more of this. Think, Sky, show us a future we'll not want to turn our faces from. Then my little boy & I take to staring at pictures of a Mars so blue we can't quite believe it & he asks about oceans there, if it's all water suddenly, he thought it was red. Didn't we all. Science—all these years—told us otherwise, told us Pluto & then no more Pluto, mapped out giants in the charted stars we accepted on faith, but it's hard to distrust our eyes that see what we're sure can only be something we know to name—*Atlantic, Pacific, Indian, Arctic.* So, I look up oceans in outer space to find that a second probe of Saturn's largest moon, Titan, discovered dry lake beds & emptied-out river channels & the name of the man who discovered that moon nearly forgotten—no constellation for him. No memorial. Elsewhere in a galaxy so large my son gets lost just thinking about it, every ocean an ocean of ice, an ocean of magma, an ocean of gas. When I show him those pictures he blinks back *that?* He stammers out *but how can the fish live there, in that? How will they swim?*

I heard, *he said he's going to make a city for all of us when we visit. He said he's going to make a city for us so we'll never want to leave.* Instead of asking for a translation, instead of trying to clarify, I said, *I would live in any city that man made,* & meant it, & when everyone stared, when everyone tried to adjust their sense of what they'd heard, I said, *think of the light there, that pulse.* Someone corrected me, annoyed, *he said dinner, not city,* & I said, *oh,* though I wasn't hearing the revision. I was thinking about where cities go when they're gone. I was thinking about the roads out of here. About how no one seems to leave with any grace. About the bowl of my body, dusting over. About predictability, how to expect something even as we can't. This slow rise. About any city our friend would make—any city whole enough—where we could live. I was thinking about our poor, damp hearts, & the ground torn up by wind that might carry us away.

A KIND OF STUTTER, THAT OVER &

over, that sometime-sound between

even the walls of our quiet
rooms, that heartbeat.

Like repeating. Like pulse.
Where we wait staring out

I thought *arson*, a word I'd never
said aloud before & then said aloud

until not a word, & you here, you
could hold a match to the debris,

could help me burn off everything.
Today brought back close-to-the-dirt

flowers my mother would snip off
& gather up & tuck in shallow

tumblers where they'd lean
far over. Brought back

my little boy being pulled from me,
his small toes tucked beneath

my ribs, & how he's still there still,
tugging the cage of my chest.

Because I don't know what to call
anything anymore, how to stop

every thing from pulling away, *arson*.
The strike of a flint. Why not? It'd all go

up, be gone, then the skies would cover
with ash & then it would start to down,

would turn to a kind of stone—
stone at our feet, stone filling

our mouths—& how days,
& everyone, would be grounded.

DOWN THE HALL THE ACCORDION MAN TURNS INTO A DOOR

he thought would open out into a corridor. He is empty-handed.
& so, when I explain to my son, wiggling in the waiting room,

how this stranger plays an instrument that most resembles one
of those stretch city buses, it sounds like a story that could be

any story. This one is true; they all are. The same day, my friend
sets a small fire in the house she's renting from you, can't recall

baking soda or powder, breaks the fan she plugs in to clear the air,
but more unbelievable, in that waiting room when I said *you were*

born here, my son's still considering how a man lost in a building
where everything is lost could be in a band harmonizing with another

man who plays spoons carried in a flute case. The pause before
he murmurs *I don't want to be born* says it's too late for these things now.

Too late. The house down the block smoky, the fabric soaking up
the smell, & everything that ends & will end sometime, & so, & so on.

of hands.   *Not* palmed against flank or curve of back, but quantifiable units. A system of measurement not relative to hand, not dependent on handler. It can't be wrong, this want of mine, for the body to be its own kind of metric, like the now-lost cubit sizing up the length from elbow to finger's tip. Or everything gauged against feet: a ruler, a dactyl, the forearm. Or a yard? Three feet, a landscaped plot of ground, storage for trains. & that hand? Four inches, even if to inch never signals distance. When my son was born every part of his body corresponded, fit right in to some part of me. Before my son was, he wedged inside me. I swear to you, measurement was first handmade. It wanted to allow room for the possibility of my palm placed, tender, along his spine, or your fingers stretching from the horse's mane to its withers.

—

BACK TO THIS WIND, UP AGAINST IT EVEN,

& the recognizable sky bearing

down this day we'd like to forget,
if forgetting were something we knew

to do, or knew to do well. Instead, in this
slouch of shoulders, in this heavy-headed

lean against palms, we'll drive fast the roads
that hold all sorrow. In this hurried-through,

only indistinguishable hours—the ones here
& the ones left to come, & the day after,

& well, you know, etcetera. The highway
a reminder. The hazy every-afternoon

a reminder. Chapped skin between fingers,
the bite of this air, the quiet settling, sweaters

unfolded & stowing away each last bit
of winter, now creased, now wrinkled, now

spread out on the bed to see what will fit, what
mothed, what frayed, or something burning off

down the street, a fireplace, a barrel, timbers where
a house once stood, all of it, calling back. Isn't

it true that once we thought we were done in, done
with broken heartness, thought, Well,

thank god for never having to feel that way again?
Now, we walk into every still room

where we once were or where we've never
been alone, or together, & think, O god,

look at the light. Even here, how we want
to say Come! Look at this. This *this* that is

really nothing. Really nothing we couldn't
see anywhere, but even branches bowing

under the weight of ice, even that city-like
glow from the traffic lights' back

& forth, their stop & go, or the factory
that must be chuffing dreams, or the way—piled

high & waiting for thaw—we were made
more forgettable, made more full of wanting

to forget, made again even smaller in this
town that's a windbreak, this town that cyclones

past everything & flattens us all. Nights we leave
the office late, turning off the building's lights, we

remember how once you & they & we & I &
time was when we didn't want to break the window glass

& throw ourselves out & down, all those stories.
If we ever live in places where we don't

count hours off by heavy machinery scraping
every single day, what then? & us? All piled up,

leaning against curbed things to be hauled away,
what of us now here or there or later, somewhere else?

Each day a new kind of grief. Not only of our own
disappearing but these days, the fraying edges of everything,

us not finding our way back. That you, you
on an airplane or in transit to someplace not here,

or snowbound & keeping time plow pass after
plow pass, you slipping away, how we might

also vanish, or vanish far enough from reach
so that—even *that* impossible—so that, even that.

early, this unmade day where small, they say, is the new big, the new black, a substitute for any modifier, made insignificant only by connotation. But we know it as verb, this sometimes prayer. Small my hands. Small our hearts in that emptying out. Small these lines, any lines. Small the boy I am trying to learn to let go. Small the bones in our feet—three called *cuneiform*—our skeletal articulations. Small these memories of other days. Small the fractures we sustain, those sometimes unbearable breaks, these rents. Small our bodies against wind, our bodies pressed against another, our bodies folding in. Small that voice, my son's near-whisper, when he talks about a bird feeder he made to hang on a tree planted small, now shading, for the baby born still before he even was. Small the *o* of my mouth when he tells it. Small this ache that remembers the call, the narrowest room all those years ago. Small the grief of each day. Small the hours without words, the hours with words. Small the winter in this rearview. Small the river so like a vein. Small the urgent pitch I feel to keep that water in sight. Small the names I know to call it, to call anything. Small what goes unsaid for years, in morning light, in any light, that muting.

WHEN MORNING WAS ALMOST UNRECOGNIZABLE AS MORNING

& the light diffused by a fog so unwinter-like we couldn't
say with certainty that this was even something close to some

variation, we thought what time had become was something
suspended, something halted like the season itself, held small

in our palms or tucked in a pocket, forgotten & then
washed, that kind of, which is not really at all but

omission—the morning an elision, winter elided, our bodies
knowing only the thin rubbings erasers leave behind. That that

morning undone by light was something far short of miracle,
we are learning this year to winter *here* means let it go—.

Means even this gauzy sky will betray. Means even our hearts
here, where the horizon goes on & on, will turn to look toward

where—in another year there'd be only white, endless for miles—
the fields are stripped bare, stilled & waiting, kept waiting.

the end of the world, or the idea of it—hard to admit,
but I've been afraid I've gotten too used to everything.

These days I don't bother with the headlines, cancelled
service for the television I can't remember how to work,

let everything again pile high. I won't even stand at the curb
when you pull away. No matter how much we dread, winter will

come & keep coming. In countries I've learned to find on the map,
people will die & keep dying. In this country where we live,

the same. There is horror & then fear. Sometimes, I'm so tired
of both, I forget they aren't the same. I would've told you

about the woman in the small room the other morning,
her two black eyes & the bones in her face—all that

broken—& the two of us pressed against the cold
wall, my arms around her, my saying *shh*, saying

it's okay now, but it's not mine to tell. What is: how
I walked into a smaller room after she walked out,

how I leaned my whole body—suddenly dizzy with rage,
with fear—against that stone wall to keep from dropping

to my knees. I should've dropped to my knees. These days
I get through pretending mostly that I forget how sad sad

can be. I know you understand. What I'm also afraid of:
it's too late to learn anything new. Too late to fix all that

we've broken. Like how we'll have to keep flooding small
towns to save bigger ones, but those cities—bowls to fill

& fill—will still drown. Like how any man could
ever raise a hand to harm. & then there's winter, that solitude

singular again. None of it more awful than any other awful.
All of it bad enough. In sadness there's no scale, & no need.

Maybe what I'm most afraid of is that when we walk out
into it all, when we hold out our arms, no one will come.

Not even birds. Not even.

starts to down—not unlike the dark these days, how it comes
all of a sudden & I'm fumbling across the room lit only by street-

lamp, feeling the walls for a switch in this still-unfamiliar where
I only sometimes remember I live. & what with the calendar

rushing toward another page, what with the layers now untucking
themselves from their stowed-away spots, Love, I'm troubling

everything: an early frost, all the fields not yet harvested, & the furnace
needing tended, & no coat in the closet to fit my not-so-little little

boy, even the flowers on the stoop not done doing what they do, & now
this coming on of quiet in these years of so much quiet. Tonight, tucked in

& fighting sleep, he says how much he likes to name things, how like
invention any word can become. When his breath slows, I'm cataloguing

what we can't get back, where we can't go back to, naming what's fallen, what
keeps falling, all the seasons that ended too soon, that never had a chance.

AT THE NEW YEAR, IN THE DARK, I WATCHED TIME

in my hand change one day to the next, then
shrugged off to bed. Because no cheeks kissed

as the hour turned, not even a whisper raised
against glasses to welcome it. So maybe, feelings

hurt, it returned the favor by leaving some kind
of mangled animal to die at the door. Maybe's what

I deserve: something once alive now in pieces
& left for me to clear away, muttering all the sorry

words I know for sorry—which sound more guilt
than apology, sound every warning in me—which really

mean *not this year either.* The last began as a bird
trapped in the basement, a starling somehow

fallen in through the chimney. Long after
I'd opened the cellar door for it to find sky,

I kept hearing its wings beating hard. For weeks,
its panic—talons on the vent-work, beak against

windowpane. Today's a clearing of snow
each hour from the steps, that kind of pile &

pileup, & the streets emptied of traffic, & everything
still as can be. It's the fourth day of the new year.

I never heard the struggle, what was left for dead,
then dead. Never heard a sound. Maybe that

will be the blessing of this year, every horror
at least silent. Maybe that.

this winter in sum: *No, thank you. I'm sorry.*
No kidding, I thought. Am I ever. Never mind

what slid through the intersection, some sedan
now on a lawn at the corner & emergency

vehicles rushing near, again, this afternoon another
slickened-over set of hours our shoulders bear into.

No thank you snow that keeps coming & coming on.
No thank you trace of accident now covered over, again.

Never mind that now, or what became of the passenger
shoved through & out & the street sign bent

beyond lean. Never mind that it's all happened
before & will keep happening. Maybe every life, in sum,

now that I think about it. I'm sorry my only fluency
in more than this language, & mostly I'm only ever

speaking to myself. I'm sorry standing at the window,
looking out into a horizon of white. I'm sorry

still pressed up against the glass, & staring. I'm sorry
the only near-prayer I whisper, sleepless, turning

over, running through the day again & again. I'm not
sorry sorry comes from sorrow, this intransitive

verb without construction, now rare, now obscure.
These days, the only thing that makes sense: sorry

its own clearing, sorry a snowdrift, sorry these days
the closest & only road left back to love, & even that

someone will plow through.

IN THIS, THIS SNOW-BRIGHTENED LIGHT OF A NEAR-SPRING MORNING, I THINK OF HIS GLASS

house not of birds, not with their loyalty, their steadfast devotion. Migration? Try this: When my father left, left behind small, symmetrical holes drilled into the floor where bolts had kept his metal bookcases from toppling, he found a lakeside condo in a high-rise built by Mies van der Rohe. I never saw from inside that skin & bones minimalism, but even now I slow, veer to stare, mouth Mies van der Rohe until even that shimmer is out of sight. My father, the collector, knew something's worth by name, by legacy. Never mind that when he left we'd only fill the holes of him practicing ugly things to say. Never mind I'd take it all back if I could, though he'd never have heard a word: my deaf father, my back turned. Why this, today? This thinking: how he must have lived before he stopped living. This thinking: I never once thought of him circling ads in a daily, the spread of his felt-tip on newsprint, those lonely months searching for a single, unencumbered space. Maybe it's this morning in this part of the city where he lived those last years without us, the snow I wake to, this sudden knowing that when we leave we leave for good— regardless the peril, regardless the light, regardless the view.

HOW QUICKLY THE BODY, WHEN ASKED, FORGETS

everything, even itself turning into &

over the left side of those days. Before the names
sieved through—our bed linens worn

soft, almost translucent—we knew how to call
back what was needed: the future

unreal conditional; the way sleep could
spread, deep around; our landscaping sky;

that plant—boxwood, rhododendron; or you,
passing this room where I fidget, hands

cupping at empty spaces around my waist
& grabbing tight this trying

to find the ease with which at rest
our arms might hold on to nothing.

STAY MOUTHED THROUGH

half sleep a decade

of mornings until even
that left, the door

slamming behind in wind
that also goes then comes again

as everything does
these days—revolving

door, boomerang,
ricochet, backfire.

Until it meant *put off*, until
it meant *defer*, until suspended

wide-awake, finally thought
leave. Years before aloud could

imagine all those rooms
going & going on

emptied out, gone. Years
should've taught well enough

there's always a departure, someone
left, someone leaving, a mess

to untangle, no words
left to ask, no need to answer.

narrowing in that yellowing dark or in the slight haze of morning,

also slight. & now what? I'd ask, if asking was something I knew
to do. Or, & then? Before the boy we'd made. Before all the years.

What held together. What came apart. The undone beginning to undo,
long before the boy. We'll remember the hotel on the Rue Sainte-Catherine,

the four-poster where we'd only slept, the glass-paneled doors
opening out over the street, or staring long at the river we couldn't

name. If now, I'd find facts for it all: depths, bedding, how wide
distance grows, any meandering stretch; if careless, how

it topples banks, how tall each wall to hold. We'll remember how
all along the river we laughed. Always that, until there wasn't. Or the cat

in the lobby of the hotel on Catherine. Or how even the boulevards
became hours that kept turning us out.

IF ALL THE LOVE WE'LL KNOW IS THE KIND OF LOVE

that smalls our angles: your hand in someone's mouth, your shoulder
in someone's mouth, your elbow in someone's whole mouth, your foot

up to the anklebone between someone's lips, maybe all love
is bigmouthed or remarkably jawed. That's probably true. Maybe

all the love we'll know is really a knowing about the remarkable ways
we open & close, hinge, unhinge. Here where I live now even

the water rattles. Not one door fits its frame. If we could forget the way
things are supposed to fold into each other—someone's cupped palm,

someone's legs & your legs, or the work of sash & sill, the work of stile &
knob & panel & goings &—. Or what's remembered: ribs & sternum

& all the windows thrown open & someone's fingers along your clavicle,
that sorrowed cage—threshold might also mean someday, mean again,

might remind that architecture's job is also one of proportion, of scale,
& in the hands of any love our bodies might set flush, might—.

BECAUSE ALL DAY THE SKY HELD BACK

what it wanted most to say, & just now, couldn't
keep its tongue, hailed down. Now

the windows & gutters, & sopping,
even the siding trembling, my mouth

turned metallic, & how the unsaid bites
through the softer parts of any hour

& tastes like disappointment,
everything undone & puddling

under the eaves where nothing stays
secret when we stand there long enough.

I'd like to say I've heard it all before, Sky,
but tonight's different, the kind of revision

almost unrecognizable, somehow. That hail
against the roofline begins to sound out

every word I could never utter aloud,
that *no matter*, that I've been done talking

for a long stretch, all that, while it keeps
repeating & repeating.

NOT ONLY THE NIGHT

vehicles, their pushing on & casting

stranger shadows on the fields, or in through
the windows of the house where I sometimes

live, or their rumble-deep
sorrow on the tracks that cross the heart

of this town, & not just that
wind here where there's nothing for it to break

against, & not just that you've left, that everyone
will leave, but that it keeps happening,

on & on, every season. Maybe
I should say, off & off, & what

the plows push against, what the night
sirens rush toward, those long trains stretching

into, their horizon the only horizon always
familiar here where the wind carries off & takes

off whatever comfort we might've found.
Not only the dark its own vehicle

for the kind of saying we can't
manage when the streetlamp's going strong,

not only that. Love, each winter we try with less:
lower the thermostat, make do with last year's

now-fraying layers, less simmering
for less time in a smaller pot on a smaller stove.

We think *just a little draft coming in.* Think we can
bear for a while whatever the wind

reduces us to for however long.
Think sometimes there's shimmer

enough to winter, maybe the promise of what
comes next, maybe the way

even the gray sky & those stark branches
pierce the light just so, & maybe

that it's hopeless enough without
our hopelessness, everything balanced

on the edge of everything. O, this tightroped
lonely. O, love—o, teetering, teetering us.

NOTES

The epigraph is from Inger Christensen's *alphabet*, translated by Susanna Nied (New Directions, 2001), with deep thanks.

"On either end of this year, on either end of every goddamn year," was inspired by the *New Yorker*'s Ben McGrath and his article "Muscle Memory" (July 30, 2007), where I first learned about proprioception and the important work at the Rehabilitation Institute of Chicago.

"Days the hours are no more fact than the unbelievable" owes thanks to a conversation with Kwame Dawes and to Evan Osnos's "Letter from Japan: Aftershocks" in the *New Yorker* (March 28, 2011).

"To scale, yes, days to scale, even when they grow so cluttered" is dedicated to Congresswoman Gabrielle Giffords.

"Just before the blood draw the other morning, I filled in small" is for the Smith family and Dean Young, and is in memory of my father.

"If there's a joke more complicated than 'knock-knock,' more" references the March 25, 1655, discovery of Titan by Dutch astronomer Christiaan Huygens.

———

For most of this heart-wrenched century, I've kept vigil with the news. For the lives lost and the lives upended, for our dear and suffering planet, and for any chance at the future, I trained myself to listen, to *not* turn away. These poems relied on the *New York Times*, the *New Yorker*, National Public Radio, the Corporation for Public Broadcasting, Reuters, the Associated Press; twenty-four-hour news cycles, the internet; *The Oxford English Dictionary*; Galesburg Public Library, Seymour Library at Knox College; countless road maps, the Burlington Northern Santa Fe line, the Chicago Transit Authority (especially the Ravenswood, now the Brown Line); the National Oceanic and Atmospheric Administration, the National Weather Service; and the Departments of Transportation in Illinois, Iowa, Indiana, Michigan, Wisconsin, and Minnesota, among others.

I'm indebted to the writing of others, daily, for this life of books stacked in so many rooms. Texts essential to this work include Cornelia F. Mutel's *A Watershed*

Year: Anatomy of the Iowa Floods of 2008; Gervase Wheeler's *Homes for the People in Suburb and Country*; a number of the Works Progress Administration's American Guide Series from the Federal Writers' Project; and Eliot Weinberger's *9/12: New York After*. Dearest writers, whose work is never far from me, include Muriel Rukeyser, Marianne Boruch, Keith Ratzlaff, Bob Hicok, Larry Levis, Nancy Eimers, Gerald Stern, Carl Phillips, Rita Dove, Ralph Angel, Marilynne Robinson, William Faulkner, James Agee, and James Baldwin. Always.

ACKNOWLEDGMENTS

Grateful thanks to the editors of the following journals, where earlier versions of these poems appeared: *Cimarron Review, Cincinnati Review, Crazyhorse, DIAGRAM, Dislocate, Grist, Hartskill Review, Hayden's Ferry Review, Hobart, Houseguest, La Fovea, Mantis, The Museum of Americana, New Orleans Review, Passages North, Quiddity, RHINO, Southeast Review, Third Coast,* and *Witness.*

"Too lazy to lip-read in noisy rooms, the other night" is included in the chapbook *Your Small Towns of Adult Sorrow & Melancholy.*

—

Thanks to Knox College for institutional support. This work was made possible, in part, due to the generosity of the John and Elaine Fellowes Fund for English and the Linda Karger Kohler Anderson Endowment, the Andrew W. Mellon Foundation's commitment to Faculty Development, and the Office of the Dean of the College. Thank you to the Department of Psychology, for motivation; to Mark Holmes, for the view from the corner of Simmons and Kellogg; and to my longtime colleagues in the English Department—Barbara Tannert-Smith, Rob Smith, Chad Simpson, Natania Rosenfeld, Nick Regiacorte, Robin Metz, Sherwood Kiraly, Gina Franco, Cyn Fitch, and Emily Anderson—for the many years. In my small pocket of this place, I feel pretty lucky. To my students, too many to name (please forgive me), in every room where we found ourselves together, and who always show me yet another way: thank you. Hannah Buckland, Alison Gaines, Meredith Noseworthy, Emily Oliver, Bryce Parsons-Twesten, Annie Pittman, Maggie Queeney, and Adam Soto: you are each here. I owe special thanks to Noah Baldino, Victoria Baldwin, and Josh Tvrdy for a quality of talk these last years from which poems are made. To Kelly Clare, a horizon of thank-yous.

In and out of so many seasons, for the kinds of conversations that somehow keep and that helped me make these poems, thank you: Carolyn and Tommaso Lesnick, Abby Factor, Keith Marran, Jen Tynes, Cassie Cross, Britta Kallmann, Audrey Petty, Beth Ann Fennelly, David Wright, Laura Adamczyk, Gretchen Henderson, Rob St. Clair, María Korol, and Alan Grostephan.

The most heartfelt thanks to Ralph Angel, Nancy Eimers, Roger Weingarten, John Mann, and especially to David Stevenson: I am still, every day, learning from you.

For early faith in this work, thank you Katie Ford, Emily Rosko, Don Bogen, Lisa Lewis, Ander Monson, Derek Mong, and Caleb Curtiss. To Jon Tribble, for trusting me and these poems, and to everyone at Southern Illinois University Press, for continually making beautiful books: thank you all for including me.

For generosity of time and spirit, true kindness, and continual inspiration, thank you Nicole Cooley and Katrina Vandenberg.

To Adrian Matejka, his careful attention, that hearing, and for getting it—I will keep saying thank you, a whole world made of thank-you.

Making poems can be pretty solitary work, so one is full of the deepest gratitude and love for the handful of people who hold off the loneliness and who keep present the present. *Nostalgia for a World Where We Can Live* would not exist without a number of dear yous. Not without my sister, Beth, and our mother, Anne, who taught me love and how to see everything, before language and in language. Not without Jeremy, for a long-ago patience and belief in me, and because there was. Not without Nick, who titled this book before I wrote a single line, poet of awe, who awes me. Not without Robin, who knew it was always about time, who still knows. Not without Ethan, who has kept the hours. Not without Beth, who makes the very best company, who is my dear reader, life raft, friend, whose poems make me a better person, and for whose long conversation—what luck!—I am unbearably and unapologetically grateful. And never without Eli, always the most tender and wise and whole person in any room, who showed me how to make a world where we could live, how to live in our world, and without whom I would have nothing to say and no reason to say it.

OTHER BOOKS IN THE CRAB ORCHARD SERIES IN POETRY

Muse
Susan Aizenberg

Millennial Teeth
Dan Albergotti

Hijra
Hala Alyan

Instructions, Abject & Fuming
Julianna Baggott

Lizzie Borden in Love: Poems in Women's Voices
Julianna Baggott

This Country of Mothers
Julianna Baggott

The Black Ocean
Brian Barker

The Sphere of Birds
Ciaran Berry

White Summer
Joelle Biele

Gold Bee
Bruce Bond

Rookery
Traci Brimhall

USA-1000
Sass Brown

The Gospel according to Wild Indigo
Cyrus Cassells

In Search of the Great Dead
Richard Cecil

Twenty First Century Blues
Richard Cecil

Circle
Victoria Chang

Errata
Lisa Fay Coutley

Salt Moon
Noel Crook

Consolation Miracle
Chad Davidson

From the Fire Hills
Chad Davidson

The Last Predicta
Chad Davidson

Furious Lullaby
Oliver de la Paz

Names above Houses
Oliver de la Paz

Dots & Dashes
Jehanne Dubrow

The Star-Spangled Banner
Denise Duhamel

Smith Blue
Camille T. Dungy

Seam
Tarfia Faizullah

Beautiful Trouble
Amy Fleury

Sympathetic Magic
Amy Fleury

Egg Island Almanac
Brendan Galvin

Soluble Fish
Mary Jo Firth Gillett

Pelican Tracks
Elton Glaser

Winter Amnesties
Elton Glaser

Strange Land
Todd Hearon

View from True North
Sara Henning

Always Danger
David Hernandez

Heavenly Bodies
Cynthia Huntington

Terra Nova
Cynthia Huntington

Zion
TJ Jarrett

Red Clay Suite
Honorée Fanonne Jeffers

Fabulae
Joy Katz

Cinema Muto
Jesse Lee Kercheval

Train to Agra
Vandana Khanna

The Primitive Observatory
Gregory Kimbrell

If No Moon
Moira Linehan

Incarnate Grace
Moira Linehan

For Dust Thou Art
Timothy Liu

Strange Valentine
A. Loudermilk

Dark Alphabet
Jennifer Maier

Lacemakers
Claire McQuerry

Tongue Lyre
Tyler Mills

Oblivio Gate
Sean Nevin

Holding Everything Down
William Notter

American Flamingo
Greg Pape

Crossroads and Unholy Water
Marilene Phipps

Birthmark
Jon Pineda

No Acute Distress
Jennifer Richter

Threshold
Jennifer Richter

On the Cusp of a Dangerous Year
Lee Ann Roripaugh

Year of the Snake
Lee Ann Roripaugh

Misery Prefigured
J. Allyn Rosser

Into Each Room We Enter without Knowing
Charif Shanahan

In the Absence of Clocks
Jacob Shores-Arguello

Glaciology
Jeffrey Skinner

Roam
Susan B. A. Somers-Willett

The Laughter of Adam and Eve
Jason Sommer

Huang Po and the Dimensions of Love
Wally Swist

Persephone in America
Alison Townsend

Spitting Image
Kara van de Graaf

Becoming Ebony
Patricia Jabbeh Wesley

Abide
Jake Adam York

A Murmuration of Starlings
Jake Adam York

Persons Unknown
Jake Adam York